Penny Rugs

Sewing Wool Appliqué

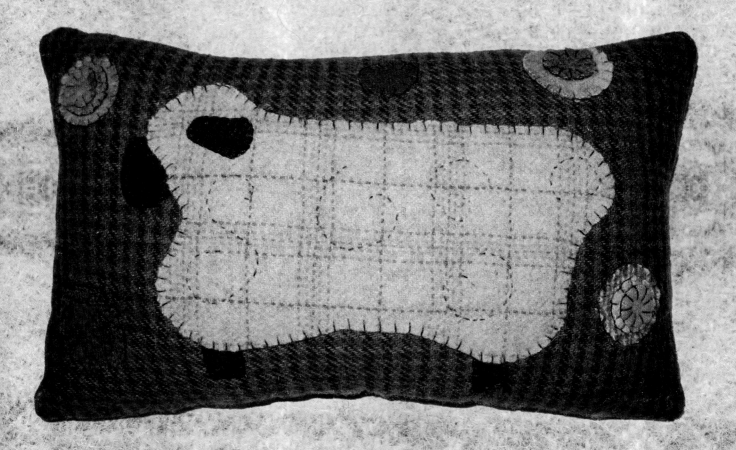

Janice Sonnen

Schiffer Publishing Ltd

4880 Lower Valley Road, Atglen, Pennsylvania 19310

Dedication

This book is dedicated to Malcolm for his love and support in all my endeavors. Also to my grandchildren, Matthew, Adrianna, Mariah, Cierra and Adelyn; may I leave them with the legacy of the joy of creating and the love of traditional crafts.

Acknowledgments

I would like to thank Sandie Painter, Tina Sonnen, the Pennsylvania German Cultural Heritage Center at Kutztown, and an acquaintance from Roanoke, Virginia, for allowing me to photograph and share their penny rugs.

Special thanks to Rachel Palmer for patience and helpfulness demonstrating the blanket stitch with her beautiful hands.

Other Schiffer Books on Related Subjects:

How to Hook Rugs. Christine J. Brault
978-0-7643-2890-9 • $14.95
Designing & Hooking Primitive Rugs. Susie Stephenson
978-0-7643-3288-3 • $14.99

Copyright © 2010 by Janice Sonnen

Library of Congress Control Number: 2009940511

Designed by Stephanie Daugherty
Type set in Swis721 BdRnd BT/Zurich BT

ISBN: 978-0-7643-3467-2

Printed in China

Schiffer Books are available at special discounts for bulk purchases for sales promotions or premiums. Special editions, including personalized covers, corporate imprints, and excerpts can be created in large quantities for special needs. For more information contact the publisher:

Schiffer Publishing Ltd.
4880 Lower Valley Road
Atglen, PA 19310
Phone: (610) 593-1777; Fax: (610) 593-2002
E-mail: Info@schifferbooks.com

For the largest selection of fine reference books on this and related subjects, please visit our web site at

www.schifferbooks.com

We are always looking for people to write books on new and related subjects. If you have an idea for a book please contact us at the above address.

This book may be purchased from the publisher. Include $5.00 for shipping. Please try your bookstore first. You may write for a free catalog.

In Europe, Schiffer books are distributed by
Bushwood Books
6 Marksbury Ave.
Kew Gardens
Surrey TW9 4JF England
Phone: 44 (0) 20 8392 8585; Fax: 44 (0) 20 8392 9876
E-mail: info@bushwoodbooks.co.uk
Website: www.bushwoodbooks.co.uk

Contents

Pennies of wool

Preface

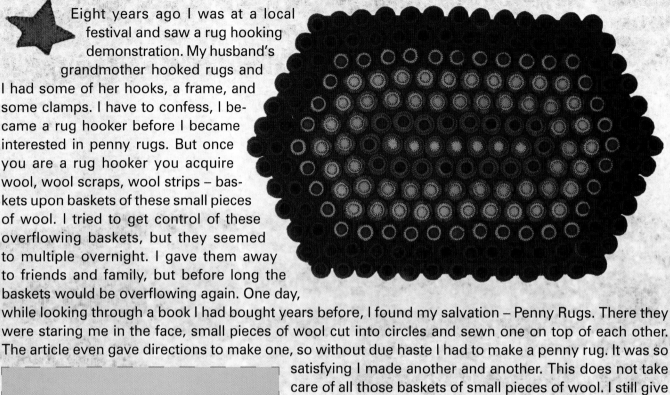

Eight years ago I was at a local festival and saw a rug hooking demonstration. My husband's grandmother hooked rugs and I had some of her hooks, a frame, and some clamps. I have to confess, I became a rug hooker before I became interested in penny rugs. But once you are a rug hooker you acquire wool, wool scraps, wool strips – baskets upon baskets of these small pieces of wool. I tried to get control of these overflowing baskets, but they seemed to multiple overnight. I gave them away to friends and family, but before long the baskets would be overflowing again. One day, while looking through a book I had bought years before, I found my salvation – Penny Rugs. There they were staring me in the face, small pieces of wool cut into circles and sewn one on top of each other. The article even gave directions to make one, so without due haste I had to make a penny rug. It was so satisfying I made another and another. This does not take care of all those baskets of small pieces of wool. I still give some away, but I don't seem to mind the full baskets anymore because somewhere in those baskets is a beautiful penny rug waiting to be made.

I feel I have been a craft person most of my life. As a child I learned to paint, knit, and sew. This extended into adulthood, only getting more sophisticated. In the 1980s I painted decorative chests and became interested in traditional crafts. My husband, Malcolm, and I live on his family farm in the Pennsylvania Dutch country in a house built in 1745. It is the house, the land, and the animals that inspire me, and the knowledge that this place has a history of generations.

After painting chests for twelve years I took a break from crafting and went back into the work force. During this time I tried my hand at quilting, but not with the passion that I found in rug hooking and later in my Penny Rugs. If you ask me which one I like the most, I would have to answer that, when I am hooking there is nothing so satisfying and when I am making a penny rug, again there is nothing so satisfying. I feel so lucky to have these two great traditional crafts at this time in my life.

This took me a whole summer of blanket stitching the pennies together, but it was well worth every minute of it, especially when I see it displayed on a table or on a chair.

History of Penny Rugs

Penny Rugs were made by rural American women in the 1800s. They were also called button or spool rugs, named after the template (pennies, buttons, or a spool) that was used for the size of the circle. Although the name, Penny Rug, implies that they were to be used on the floor, they were actually used on tables or other furniture and not on the floor. The term "rug or rugg" was meant as coverlets for beds. We do not know when "rug" started to be referred to and used as a floor covering. The women who made these rugs in the very beginning wanted to brighten their homes, and what better way than to use scrapes of material that were still serviceable from clothing and blankets?

Pennies are graduated circles that are sewn on top of each other with the blanket stitch. Circles weren't the only designs that were used. Birds, trees, animals, stars, and flowers were used as these were things in everyday life. Penny Rugs with primarily circles were made around the end of the Civil War and more ornate Penny Rugs were made throughout the Victorian area. In the early 1900s, textile factories emerged and the Penny Rugs seemed to take a back seat to factory made items. They have made a comeback and are growing in popularity.

These are actual pennies from the 1800s. These pennies are much bigger than ours, measuring 1 1/8 inches. I wonder if any of these pennies were ever used to make a penny rug?

Left: **This antique rug is in the textile collection at the Pennsylvania German Cultural Heritage Center in Kutztown. It has single pennies that have been appliquéd with wool stars, flowers, clover, etc. The edge of the rug is bound in red cotton fabric and is backed with burlap. It measures 45 X 24.75 inches.**

This a fine late 19th or early 20th century Pennsylvania German tongue rug with pennies. The tongues have been bound with material instead of using the blanket stitch. Each tongue has been accented with an embroidered star pattern.

Notice the cross-stitch pattern around the edge of the penny rug. The pennies have been done with an assortment of colors. This penny rug also comes from the collection of the Pennsylvania German Cultural Heritage Center in Kutztown.

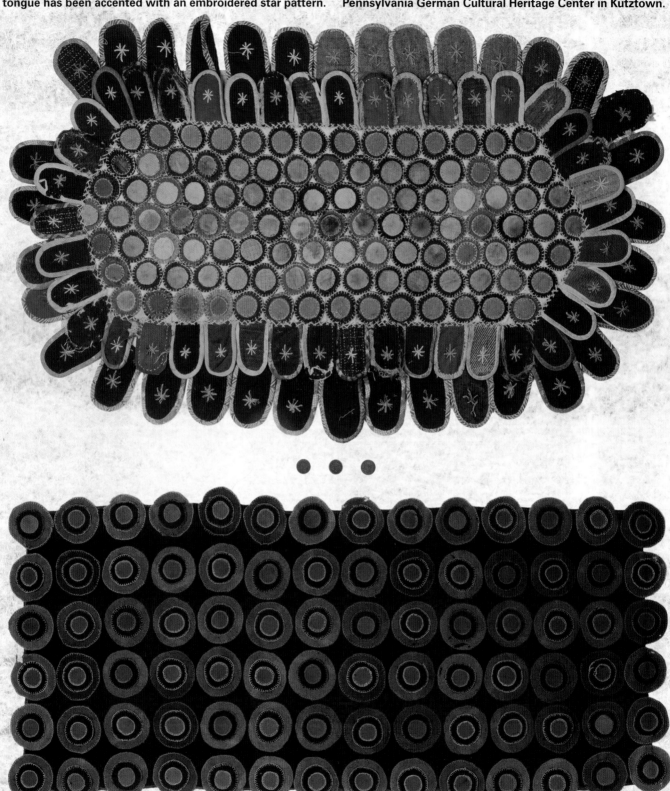

This is an antique rug from the late 1800s. The owner purchased the rug in 1998 or 1999 in Radford, Virginia. Many Germans, English, and Scottish people traveled down the Shenandoah Valley from Pennsylvania and other

English and Scots came across the mountains from coastal Virginia, so the exact history of the rug is unknown. This penny rug is in very good condition considering its age. The colors have held wonderfully.

What You Need

Many of the things you need to make a penny rug are probably already in your home. You may even find an old wool shirt or coat that would make great pennies.

Most people love the feel of wool. It is soft, warm, and very comforting.

Wool is the best material for a Penny Rug, but if you don't have a supply of wool, craft felt can be used. In fact, my very first Penny Rug was made out of craft felt and it has held up fairly well. I buy new wool in yardage, but remember I am also a rug hooker and need more wool than for a Penny Rug. If you buy wool from a second hand store, take it home and felt it, by washing it in hot water with ¼ cup of detergent, before you take it apart. This helps prevent a lot of fraying. I also felt new wool. This brings the fibers together, fluffs the wool, and helps with fraying. After washing the wool I throw it into the dryer with an old towel. I prefer to use medium weight wool. Coat wool, which is the heaviest wool, is also great for pennies. Wash all the colors separately since colors may fade in the hot water. I like to use texture wools (wools that are a small plaid or have other colors running through them).

Pins: Long shank pins with plastic heads

Perle Coton: #5 or #8 in black or contrasting colors. Perle Coton #5 is a heavier thread and accents your pennies very nicely. If you are using wool that frays a little, this is the thread to use. Perle Coton #8 is good when you don't want to call too much attention to the stitching but nevertheless it still makes a statement. This is available at craft stores.

Sewing needle: A tapestry needle is a needle with a large eye and the Perle Coton will go through it easily.

Freezer paper: This is found in a grocery store near the other food wraps. It is a flat white on one side and shiny on the other side. Freezer paper is great for tracing all your circles. You will use the flat side to trace on. The shiny side will stick lightly to your wool when ironed on, making it easy to cut out your "pennies." These freezer paper circles peel off the wool easily and can be reused many times, until there is so much wool fuzz on them that they won't stick any more. I keep them in little plastic bags with the size of the circle written on the bag. After ironing on the circles, it's time to cut them out. This may seem tedious but is so satisfying to see the stacks of circles.

You can use almost any type of thread for a penny rug. My favorite is Perle Coton.

Pen or marker: It does not have to be permanent marker. This is for making circles on the freezer paper.

Templates: Coins, candlesticks, drinking glasses, anything round. Find at least three objects that are graduated in size.

Patterns: This is the first thing you must decide before making a Penny Rug. Diamonds were the most popular **in the 1800s.** Circles, rectangles, squares, and hexagons were also used. You will also need to determine how big or how small you are going to make your Penny Rug. Next you will need to determine the size of your pennies and if your pennies are going to be two or three pennies high.

Color: Back in the 1800s they didn't worry about colors, they used what they had left from their clothing and blankets. Try to use colors that complement each other and use colors that you like. If you don't know what colors to use, look around your home, look at what colors you decorate with and what colors you like to wear.

Sewing the Penny Rug

When I started to make Penny Rugs I always forgot how to start the Blanket Stitch. Remember to always come up from the bottom and you will not have a problem.

The blanket stitch is the most popular stitch to use on your Penny Rugs. It is a fairly easy stitch and helps keep the wool from fraying. With your needle threaded with Perle Coton and a knot at one end, bring it up through the material from the bottom. Move about a quarter of an inch to the right and take a stitch into the top circle about one-fourth inch wide, catching the bottom circle as you take this stitch. After taking the stitch, catch the thread and pull it until the thread frames the top circle. Continue to do the blanket stitch completely around the top penny. If you are doing three layers of pennies, attach the top two onto the third or bottom circle.

Move a quarter of an inch to the left inserting the needle into the bottom penny and come up a quarter of an inch into the top penny.

You will now go a quarter inch and following the same pattern make your next blanket stitch.

A loop forms with the Perle Coton. You will go through this loop and as you pull the thread through you will have formed your first Blanket Stitch. You will see that the Perle Coton lays right alongside your penny.

You will do this stitch until you have gone completely around your penny.

To end the blanket stitch, pull your needle and thread to the back, right alongside your first stitch, and knot it.

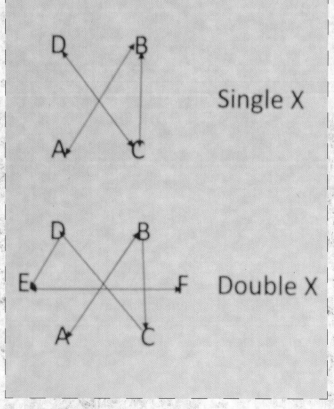

Before joining my circles I sometimes will embroider some stitching on top of the first or smallest circle. This is usually a single X or a double X. These are flat stitches. They are decorative stitches and could be done in corresponding colors of the Perle Coton. You can also accent the top penny by making your blanket stitch a half inch wide instead of one-fourth inch wide. Larger, single layer pennies can even be more ornate. Different types of embroidery stitches can be used on these larger, single layer pennies.

A simple accent to the top penny adds interest to your Penny Rug.

Single X

Double X

Coming up from the bottom a single or double X is easy to stitch following the diagram.

You can also accent your penny top by taking a longer stitch, 0.5 to .75 of an inch into the center of the penny.

Constructing a Penny Rug

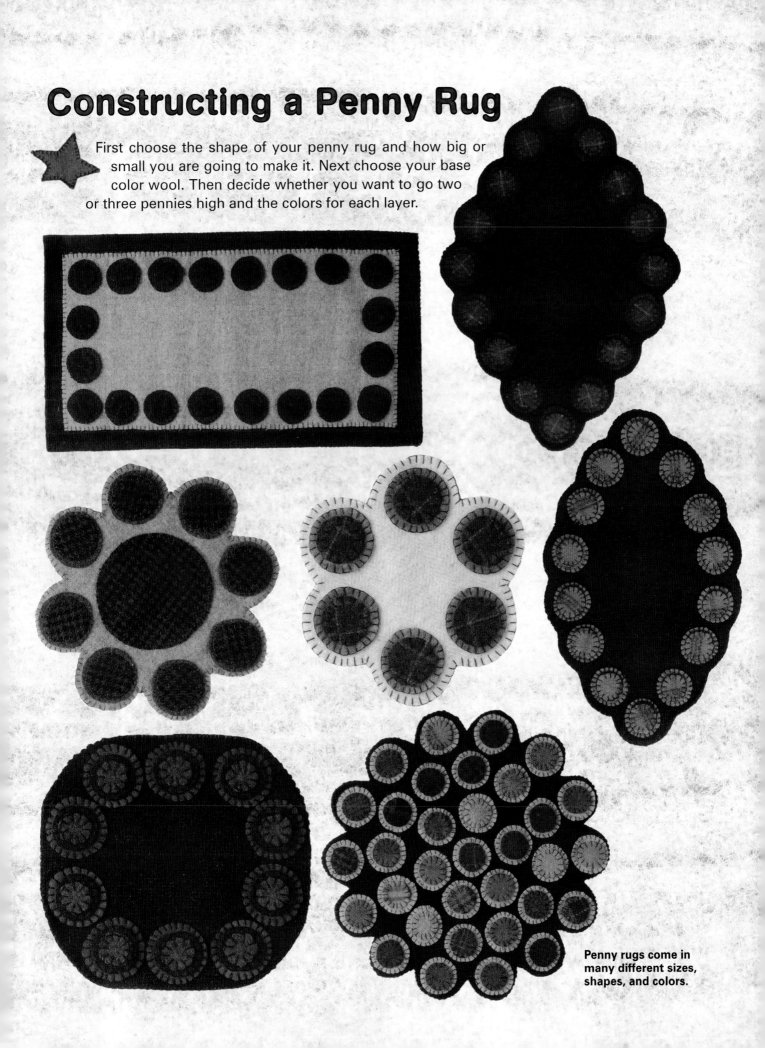

First choose the shape of your penny rug and how big or small you are going to make it. Next choose your base color wool. Then decide whether you want to go two or three pennies high and the colors for each layer.

Penny rugs come in many different sizes, shapes, and colors.

1. After figuring out how many pennies you will need for your rug trace your template onto the dull side of the freezer paper. If you need fifteen pennies for your rug, you are going to trace fifteen circles for each penny layer. If the bottom layer is going to be blue, the medium penny red and the smallest penny white, you will need fifteen pennies of each color of wool.

Freezer paper comes in handy in the making of penny rugs. It is easy to work with and very economical.

When first using the freezer paper circles trace and cut them in groups of five. This makes it easier to iron the circles onto the wool strip and you don't have to cut each individual circle out of the freezer paper and then out of wool.

2. Iron the strips of freezer paper pennies onto your strips of wool and cut out the circles. This is tedious but so worth the time.

The freezer paper pennies can be used many times. After being ironed onto the wool they will stick and will make it easier to cut out a nice round penny. I try to make a perfect circle but they are hand cut and sometimes, no matter how hard I try, I cannot cut the perfect circle.

3. Start by sewing the smallest pennies to the medium pennies with the blanket stitch. Then you stitch these two layers to the largest penny with the blanket stitch. I like to blanket stitch all my pennies for the rug first and then pin them to the base wool. After pinning them in place, start blanket stitching the largest penny to the base wool. You can now see how your penny rug is going to look.

If you are not adding any tongues you can blanket stitch the two base wools together.

After blanket stitching your pennies together, whether they are just two or three pennies high, start positioning them on your base cloth. When you are satisfied with their placement, pin them in place.

The fun begins when you actually start stitching you pennies to the base cloth.

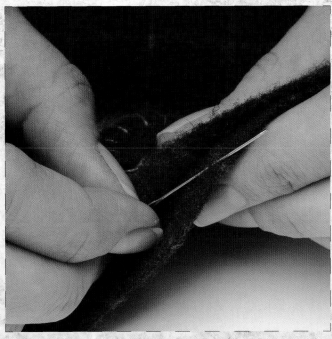

To start blanket stitching around the end of your rug, knot one end of your Perle Coton and make a small stitch between the two base wools to hide the knot and then start the blanket stitch. *(Top Right)*

No matter whether you are sewing a penny or finishing your rug with the blanket stitch, it is started the same way. When finishing your penny rug the first stitch is made inside or between the top and the bottom of the penny rug.

To change to a new strand of Perle Coton while going around your rug, stop stitching when you have at least two inches of Perle Coton left on your needle. You will take a stitch over your last blanket stitch, go between the base wool, and sew two small stitches to anchor your Perle Coton. Start the new strand by coming up between the base wool as you did in the beginning, coming up where you made the last blanket stitch.

4.

1.

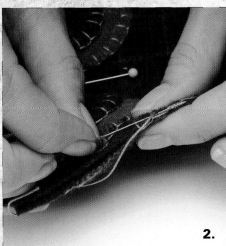

2.

3.

1. When ending a thread, go over the last stitch. 2. Then take two little stitches over and around the next two blanket stitches to anchor your thread. 3. To start a new strand of thread, come up from inside your rug right alongside your last blanket stitch. 4. The blanket stitch around the edge of your penny rug gives it a very nice finished accent.

The Scalloped Rug

A scalloped base wool is done when you design your rug. The pattern itself is drawn with the scallops and then cut. When you are cutting the scallops it is easier and you will get a nicer cut scallop if you go in two different directions while cutting. First cut half of the scallop to the right, proceeding to cut all the right sides of the scallop around the rug. Next go the left side of the scallop and cut the second half of the scallop. It is easier to cut the scallops this way instead of trying to cut down in the valley of each scallop. The blanket stitching on a scallop rug is also a little different. Always try to get one stitch down in the scallop valley to make sure it is fully anchored.

Eight double penny scallops are so practical. They can be used under lamps, candles, as a hot pad, and under a plant.

The scalloped edging is not an added piece of wool, it is done by cutting your base cloth into scallops.

When cutting scallops it is easier first to cut to the right, cutting all of the right sides of the scallops first.

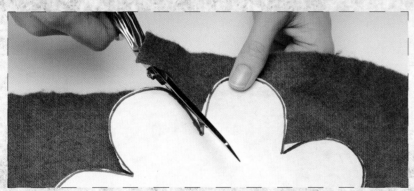

After all the right sides have been cut, start cutting the left side of the scallops.

A stitch into the center of the scallop valley secures the front to the back.

These are sixteen double penny scallop mats. They can be used in the middle of a table, a side table, or on a dresser.

Overhanging Pennies

Overhanging pennies are pennies that go beyond the edge of the base cloth and only half of the penny is attached to the base. After sewing the pennies together with the blanket stitch you are ready to attach the first row of pennies along the edge. The base wool needs to be lying flat on a table so you can pin the pennies in their correct place. When sewing the top penny or two pennies to the largest penny, make sure you have enough Perle Coton to go around the whole penny. This way you only have one knot to hide on the base wool. Check your pennies after you have them pinned so you don't have any knots in the overhang. When blanket stitching these pennies to the base wool you only sew half of them to the base wool but continue blanket stitching the penny. After sewing all the pennies onto the base wool, place this onto the back piece of the base wool and blanket stitch from the back.

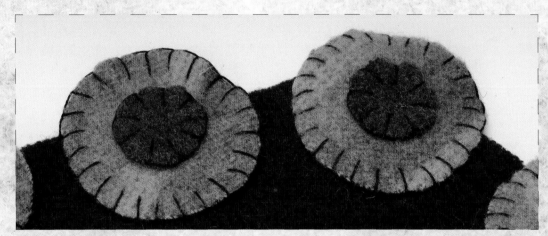

Overlying pennies may make your rug look like a scalloped rug but only half of the penny is attached.

1. When placing and pinning an overlying penny at the edge of your base wool, less than half of your penny lies beyond the base wool.

3. Blanket stitching is the same on the overlying penny, you are just sewing a single layer of wool where the penny overlies.

2. From sewing your pennies together you will have a knot on the pennies' back. This part of the penny should be placed on the base cloth so it does not show.

4. The back base wool is placed on top of the front of the penny rug and you will stitch these two together from the back.

Applying Tongues

Tongues are use for a border on your rug. You can place them around your rug or, if it is a rectangle rug, just at both ends of the rug. To make a tongue you will cut out two pieces of your desired shape for each tongue. You can also use a single tongue, but I like the weight of a double tongue as a border as it will lay better.

Before blanket stitching the tongues together you may want to add one or two layers of graduating tongues, or add a penny onto the top tongue. Another embellishment is an embroidery stitch on the top tongue. Then blanket stitch them together. After completing the top of your rug and your tongues you will place the back of the base wool down on a table and pin the tongues in place with the head of the pin sticking outward. Place the finished penny rug on top and pin in place. You will first blanket stitch all around the top of the penny rug, going between the tongues and catching the tongues as you blanket stitch. After completing the top, turn the penny rug over and you will see the back of each tongue still needs to be stitched. You will blanket stitch the back of each tongue.

With tongues all around this oval, it is ready for the holidays with dark red and brown plaid and red pennies. A close up reveals the accent stitch on the tongues.

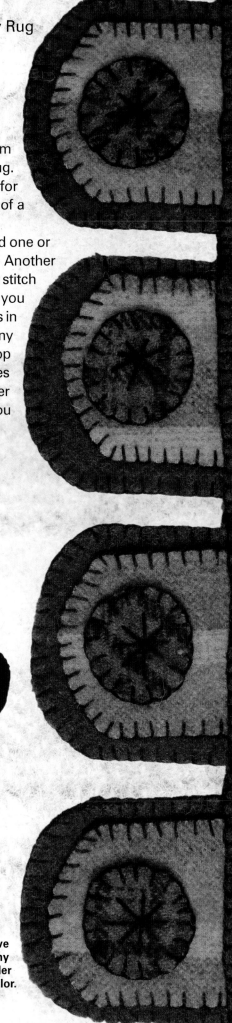

A close up of tongues that have an accent stitch on the penny and have a light colored, smaller tongue on the base color.

Constructing a Penny Rug

1. A tongue is two cut tongues blanket stitched together after adding any embellishments.
2. The head of the pin should be sticking outwards so you can pull it out after you have stitched your rug together. 3. You can see from this picture that the back of the tongues are not finished and they still need to be blanket stitched. 4. You now have a sandwiched rug, the finished top, the tongues, and the bottom.

Labeling Your Penny Rug

The last thing you should do to your Penny Rug is to place a label on the back. A piece of muslin or other plain material and a fine permanent marker will do. You can write something about the wool, such as where the wool came from or where or why you made the rug. Also make sure to add your name and the date to this label. Remember these are tomorrow's heirlooms and future generations will want to know who made them and when they were stitched.

A label is important for future generations. You can place the label anywhere on the back of your rug.

The Art of Dyeing Wool

When I am at a show demonstrating a Penny Rug or rug hooking I am always asked if I dye my own wool. I do dye a small percent, but use more "as is wool" because I feel the wool that I am buying oftentimes is so beautiful and already has a dyed look to it. Dyeing wool is fun and I encourage you to try it. I dye wool as simply as I can and usually get good results. There are several methods of dyeing wool and if you experiment with other methods, you will find one that you are most comfortable with.

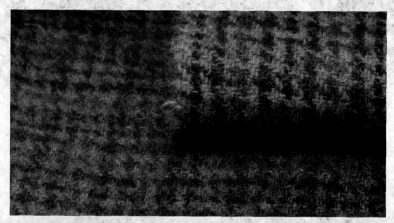

A light green and red tweed (the one on top) turns into a blue-green wool using Jack Boy Blue recipe.

Dyeing wool can be fun and interesting with the right equipment.

Equipment for dyeing

Enamel or stainless steel pot: I found a large enamel pot at a secondhand store and that seems to be my favorite. One thing of utmost importance is to keep you dye pots separate from your kitchen pots. In fact, store them out of the kitchen so no one else ever thinks about using them for preparing food.

Cushing™ Acid Dyes: These dyes come in a large range of colors.

Measuring spoons: Cushing has special spoons and, if you are planning to dye quite a bit of your wool, I would suggest purchasing these spoons.

Rubber gloves: You want to protect your hands when you dye wool.

Wooden spoon: This is to stir your dye into the water.

Salt, uniodized: Salt helps distribute the dye and give you an even dyed color.

White vinegar: to set the color in your wool.

After gathering your equipment it is time to start your dye bath. First put the wool you want to dye (usually a half yard at a time) into another pot or basin filled with warm water and a little bit of detergent and let this soak for at least a half hour. Next fill your enamel pot at least three-fourths full and put it on the stove on high and bring the water to a boil. You can add 1 tablespoon of salt to this water.

When the water starts to boil take a cup full of boiling water out of the pot (using a glass mixing cup that you will always keep separate from your kitchen measuring cup) and add your dye to this water and mix. Add this cup of dye and water to your dyeing pot and stir with a wooden spoon. Make sure there are no little particles that haven't been dissolved.

You are now ready to add your wool. Wring the excess water out of the soaking wool and add it to the dye bath. Turn the stove's heat down and simmer the wool for 20-30 minutes.

The dye will be absorbed into the wool and the water will start to look clear. At this time, add about one-fourth cup of vinegar and stir. Simmer for another ten minutes and if the water doesn't clear add another one-fourth cup of vinegar.

When the water has cleared I carefully take the wool out of the pot placing it into a basin of lukewarm water and start to cool it. When the wool is cool I rinse it and then place it in my washing machine to spin the rest of the water out of the wool. I then dry it in the dryer with an old towel.

My favorite Cushing Dye is Khaki Drab as this seems to tone down a lot of bright colored wool. If you would like to dye your wool and need formulas for different colors, I would suggest that you purchase one or several books on dyeing. My favorite is *Antique Colours for Primitive Rugs* by Emma Lou Lais and Barbara Carroll.

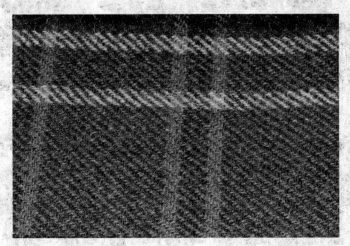

I did not care for this big, bold plaid once I bought it and brought it home. I put it aside to over dye it. I absolutely loved the three shades I got once it was over dyed.

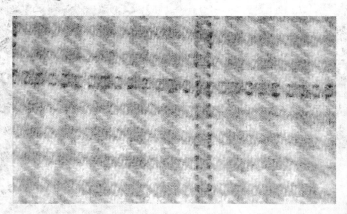

Light colored wool is wonderful for dyeing. Here is beige before and after it is dyed a wonderful golden color. I used the recipe for Neat Gold from Antique Colours for Primitive Rugs for this great color.

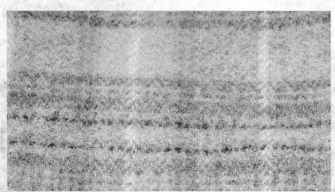
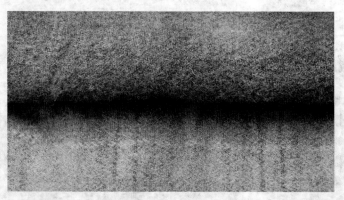

Light colored plaids will give added interest to your wool after dyeing. The beige plaid after dyeing has turned into a wonderful mottled blue and a gold with plaid lines turning darker. Recipes are Neat Gold and Jack Boy Blue.

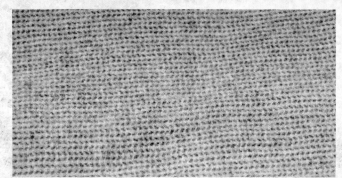

Wool that has a two tone weave to it is extra special once it is dyed. The light gray turned into a mottled green with black specks using Bronze Green and the dark burgundy dye called Hooked on Reds hardly shows any black specks at all.

This wool looks just like oatmeal and dyes almost any color with ease. Different shades of oatmeal make a wonderful addition to your stash of wool.

Two Penny Rug Artists

Tina Sonnen, my daughter-in law, is an emerging Penny Rug artist. Even though she is very busy with baby Adelyn and helping my son with a herd of Holsteins, she still manages to find time for her creative side. Her Penny Rugs are exquisitely different in style. She dyes wool to make the colors very old looking and her style is very unique. She loves to over-dye her wool (dye one color overtop of another) and her choices of colors are very subtle and endearingly close to nature. She is constantly looking for ways to improve, whether it is her dyeing methods, the thread she uses, or her patterns. She occasionally will display her wares at shows. The Weathervane Shop at Landis Valley Museum also has some of her Penny Rugs in their shop. Hopefully in the future people will be able to enjoy more of Tina's work.

This is a very unique penny rug which has been sewn with whole and half pennies. If you look closely Tina did not just cut a penny in half but each half of a penny is uniquely different. Another interesting and creative example of this penny rug is the twisted strip of wool forming a square for the center.

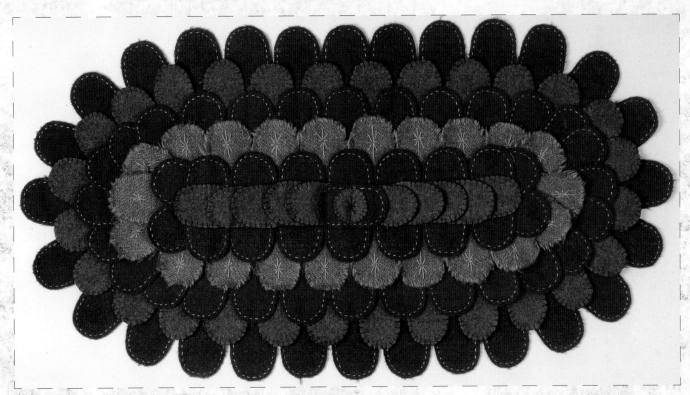

Tina Sonnen has made this very complicated tongue rug in alternating colors of gold and green. The gold tongues were cut and then washed so they would fray. They were then accented with the star stitch. There are one hundred and thirty-five tongues in this rug and it has been backed with corresponding wool.

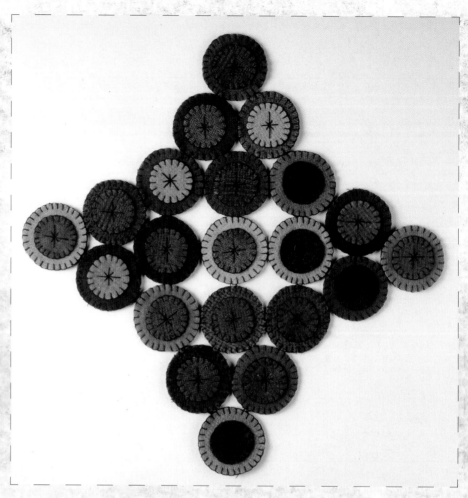

Tina Sonnen's hand dyed, multicolored diamond shape penny rug has not been sewn on a base cloth. Tina has connected them by stitching them together at strategic points of the pennies. She has also placed a star shape accent stitch on the top penny.

I included Tina Sonnen's star penny to show you that penny rugs do not need to be square, rectangular, or a diamond. She has single and double pennies filling the star with accents of stitching.

Sandie Painter does very traditional and historically correct Penny Rugs. Sandie has been making rugs since 1995. She creates hand-sewn rugs, hearth rugs, and penny rugs. Her rugs depict her own variations of historical designs. She likes to use natural dyes such as tansy, marigolds, elderberry, and dyer's chamomile. She experiments with various plants, as would have been done by the women of the 1800s. Her business card expresses her true feeling of her craft "guided by the past, connecting the generations".

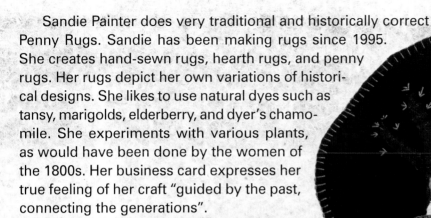

Sandie Painter says the inspiration for this rug was the Yellow Barn at Landis Valley Museum in Lancaster County, PA. There are many weddings held in the Yellow Barn and the wreath is in preparation for an upcoming wedding. The yellow wool was dyed at Landis Valley Museum, over an open fire, iron kettle using Dyer's Chamomile Flower as the dye. Sandie also uses a label on the back of the rug with information about the rug.

A story rug by Sandie Painter. A story rug often told stories to the next generation; to learn of a family's heritage. This rug is based on two scriptures in the Bible, Job.38.7 and Psalm 107.29 – "morning stars sang together – He stilled the storm to a whisper."

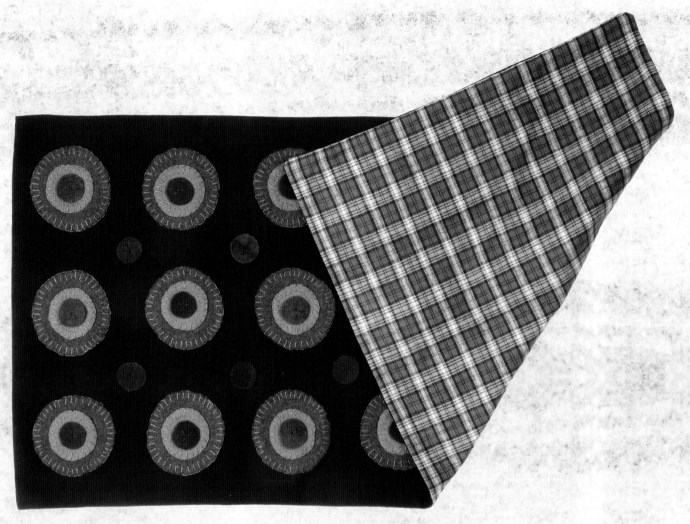

This rug, made by Sandie Painter, was inspired by the traditional Penny-Spool Rug. The center circle on this pieced was dyed in the 19th Century method, over an open fire, in an iron kettle, using black walnuts as the dye. They used what they had on hand and sometimes one circle might be different-can you locate it! Also, this rug has been backed with flannel.

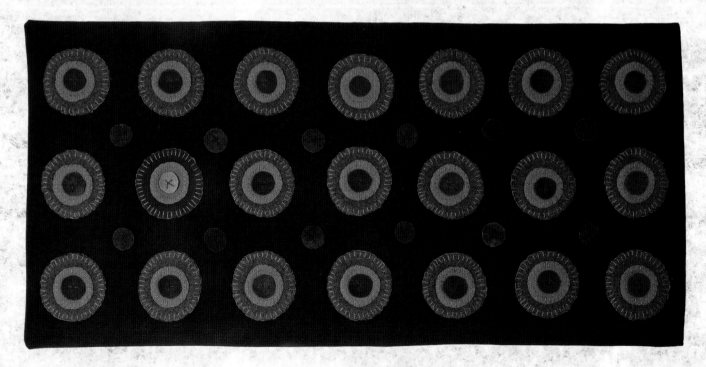

Penny Rug Projects

Mug and Candle Rugs

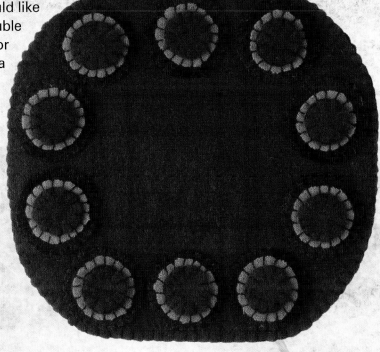

The first types of Penny Rugs I would like to introduce you to are simple double penny rugs used as Mug Rugs or Candle rugs. They can be made in a very short time with a small amount of wool. These rugs are nice hostess gifts, wrapped around a set of candles or in a special cup with some herbal teas.

Oval Candle Penny Rug
8 X 7.5 inches

Materials needed:

Two bases (See pattern on Page 64)

Ten 1 ¾ inch circles

Ten 1 ¼ inch circles

Ten 1 inch circles

Black Perle Coton or a contrasting color of Perle Coton.

Follow the general instructions for blanket stitching the pennies, attaching them to your base cloth, and attach the front to the back.

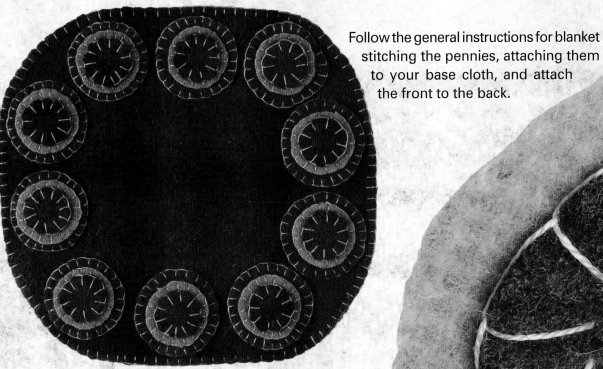

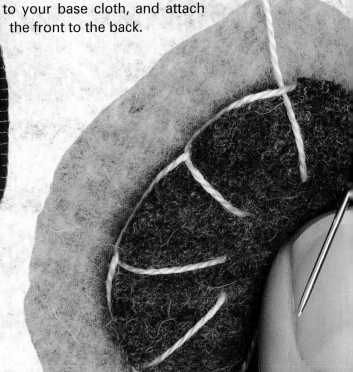

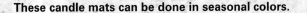

These candle mats can be done in seasonal colors.

Scalloped Edged and Overlying Penny Rugs

Six penny, Scalloped Mug Penny Rug

This has only two layers of pennies. It measures 6.5 X6.5.

Materials needed:

Two bases (See patterns on pages 56 & 57

Six 1 ¾ inch circles

Six 1 ¼ inch circles

Black Perle Coton or a contrasting color of Perle Coton #8.

So quick and easy to stitch, these six double penny mug rugs are an inexpensive gift to give to co-workers or as an appreciation gift.

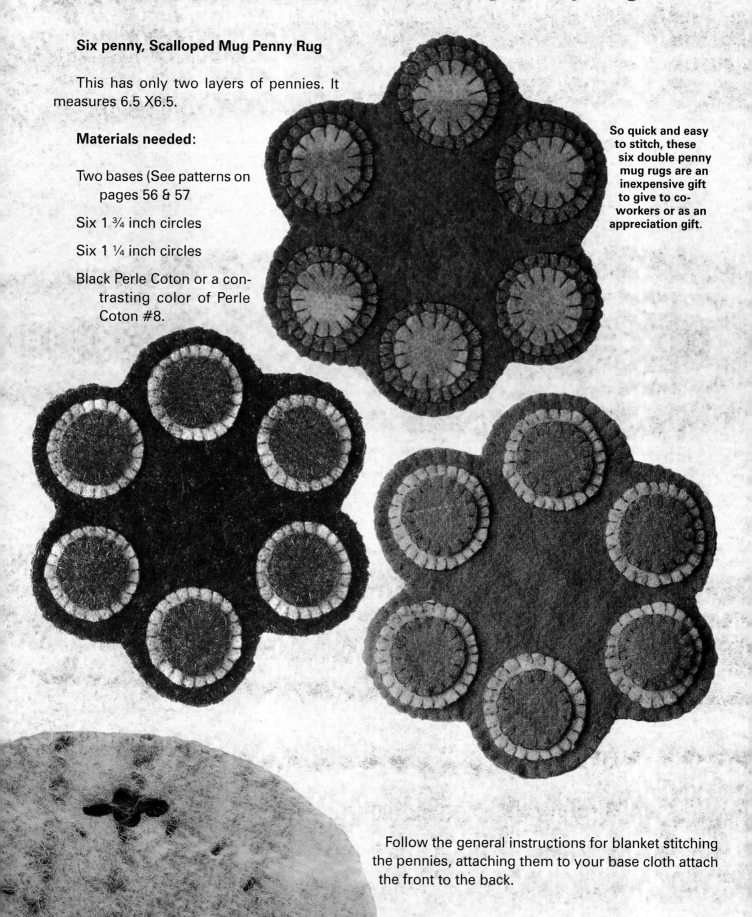

Follow the general instructions for blanket stitching the pennies, attaching them to your base cloth attach the front to the back.

Oblong Scalloped Candle Mat

This measures 14.5 X 9 inches. Cut a top and a back for your rug with the pattern already containing the scallops. As you finish your rug you will blanket stitch around the scallops as you would for any other rug. Scallops are not hard, but make sure to make a stitch in the valley between each scallop to anchor the back to the top.

If you want to make a multi-colored rug. You would cut 14 large circles out of one color but cut 14 circles out of 14 different colored wools.

Materials needed:

Two scalloped bases (See pattern on Page 55)

Fourteen 1 ½ inch circles

Fourteen 1 inch circles

Black Perle Coton #5

Follow the general instructions for blanket stitching the pennies, attaching them to your base cloth and how to attach the front to the back.

These penny rugs illustrate the different colors and the number of scallops used to make your penny rugs look different.

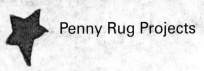

Diamond Shaped Overlying Penny Rug

This measures 14 X 10 and was done with overlapping pennies. I have also accented the pennies by using a contrasting Perle Coton and by taking a half-inch blanket stitch on the large and small pennies. The pennies in the center are single pennies and I have also accented them with contrasting Perle Coton and with the half-inch stitch. This is done with two different colors of wool and I will refer to them as Wool Color One and Wool Color Two.

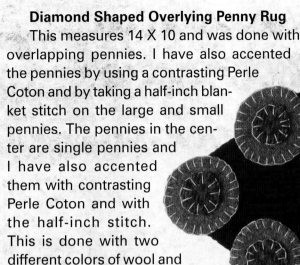

This diamond shaped penny has overlying pennies and just a single penny in the center. The gold wool is very stunning against the black background.

Materials needed:

Two diamonds bases (See pattern on Page 54)

Wool color #1: twelve 2 inch circles

Wool color #1: nine 1 inch circles

Wool color #2: twelve 1 inch circles

Perle Coton #8.

I consider this my after-the-Civil War Penny Rug. The pennies are done in very muted colors of a dark camel, brown plaid, and a uniform blue. The base is army blanket green. It has forty-seven triple pennies. The outer pennies overlie the base wool.

Remember, on an overlapping penny you only attach half of your circle, but continue blanket stitching around the full penny. Also, check to see that the knot underneath your pennies is not seen in the overlapping penny. To apply your backing, stitch it from the back with the blanket stitch, catching the back side of the overlapping penny as you go around the back.

Overlying pennies of red, gold and blue on a blue plaid background looks wonderful on a table during the summer months.

Penny Rugs with Tongues

Tongues are a unique way to accent your Penny Rug. They can either go all around your rug or simply be at the end of a rectangular rug. Rectangular rugs with tongues make great table runners. Tongues can be of the same color as the base wool or of a contrasting color, maybe the same color as one of the pennies.

Rectangular Penny Rug with Tongues

Materials needed:

Two 20 X 11 inch base pieces.

Twenty 2 inch circles

Twenty 1 inch circles

Twelve 3 ¼ X 2 ¾ inch tongues (see pattern Page 53

Sew all of your pennies and tongues together. Blanket stitch your pennies to your base wool Place your backing wool down first and position the tongues in place, placing approximately ½ inch of the tongue onto the backing. You can pin these in place by placing pins so you can pull them out once the rug is stitched. Next, place the finished top of your penny rug in place and pin between the pennies. Blanket stitch completely around the rug, catching the tongues with the blanket stitch as you go around. When you are finished blanket stitching the top, turn the rug over and blanket stitch the back of the tongues.

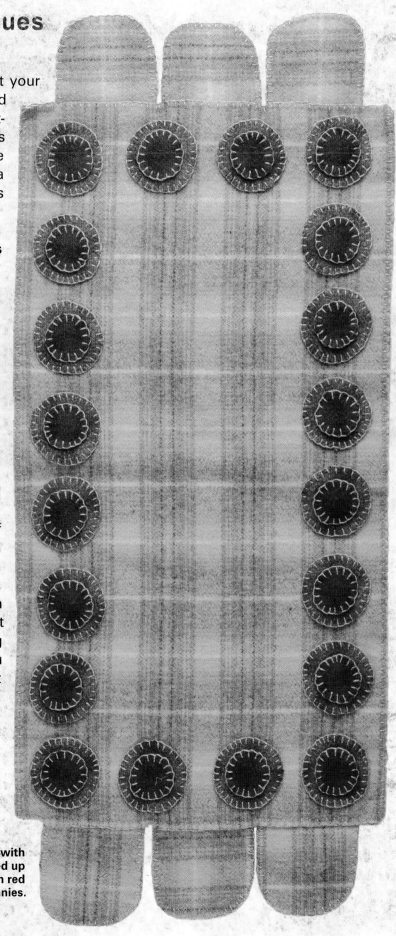

A table runner with tongues all dressed up for the holidays with red and green pennies.

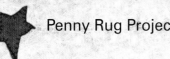

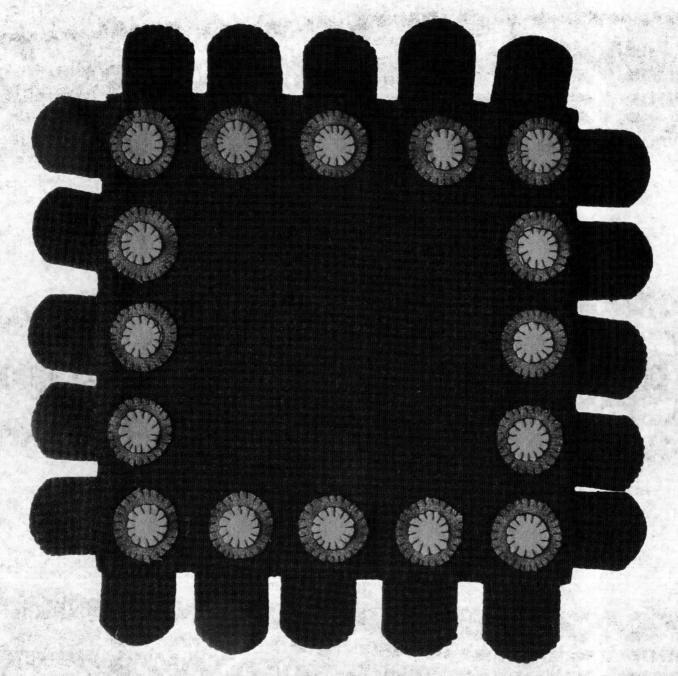

Square Penny Rug with Tongues

A penny rug with tongues on all four sides is used in the middle of a large table or a smaller table with the tongues hanging over the edge.

Materials needed:

Two 15 X 15 inch base pieces

Sixteen 2 ¼ inch circles

Sixteen 1 ³/₈ inch circles

Forty 2 ½ X 2 ¼ inch tongues

Perle Coton: Black #5.

Finishing your Penny Rug following the directions for the rectangular Penny Rugs.

Challenging Penny Rugs

The following rugs are challenging, not because they are hard but because there are so many pennies. It will give you a great amount of satisfaction once you are finished with this type of Penny Rug and it will be so beautiful. As you look at a geometric rug you will see the lines and angles. If you look closer you will see all the pennies are in rows no matter which way you look at it.

Hexagon Penny Rug

Materials needed:

Two hexagons from a 36 X 30 inch piece
of wool

Thirty-seven 2 ¼ inch circles

Thirty-seven 1 ¾ inch circles

Thirty-seven 1 ⅜ inch circles

Three skeins of Perle Coton #5.

To show the different shapes of a Penny Rug I did this hexagon rug of thirty-seven triple pennies. It takes time to sew all the pennies together but there is so much satisfaction when the last penny has been sewn to the base wool.

After cutting and blanket stitching all of your circles, start to place them on the top piece of base wool. Start by placing them across the center of the rug, seven should fit with the edge pennies overlying the base wool. The next row on either side of the center will hold six pennies, the next row five and the outer edge of the penny rug holds four.

You may have to play with the placement until the pennies are in rows. Pin all the pennies in place but as you stitch be careful of all the pins. Start stitching the outer pennies first and work to the center. Remember the outer pennies are overlying pennies and are only stitched onto the base wool half way and then continue to blanket stitch the rest of the penny. Be sure to check where your knots under the pennies are placed so they will not be seen when the rug is turned over.

Table Runner

This rug contains 115 triple pennies or 345 pennies. So if you really want a challenge, this is the rug for you. It contains four different wools for the pennies and the color sequence of these four wools change in each row.

Materials needed:

Wool Color #1:- Gold. – 60 X 8 inch piece of wool.

Wool Color #2-Blue.- 60 X 8 inch piece of wool.

Wool Color #3-Light Plaid- 36 X 8 inch piece of wool.

Wool Color #4-Red. 60 X 2 inch strip of wool.

Wait to cut the wool for the top and bottom bases of the approximately 33 X 17 table runner base until all the pennies are stitched and pinned in place. This way you can play a little with the pennies and the space between each penny.

Forty-nine 2 inch gold circles

Sixty-six 2 inch blue circles

Twenty-five 1 $\frac{5}{8}$ inch blue circles

Fifty-nine 1 $\frac{5}{8}$ light plaid circles

Thirty-six 1 $\frac{5}{8}$ gold circles

Fifty-four 1 $\frac{1}{4}$ inch red circles

Seven 1 $\frac{1}{4}$ inch light plaid circles

Twenty-four 1 $\frac{1}{4}$ inch blue circles

Thirty 1 $\frac{1}{4}$ inch gold circles

At least four skeins of #5 Perle Coton

Pattern Placement: Row 1 is the center of the rug. Subsequent rows go completely around this first row. I know it can be confusing but look at the placement of the colors in the photo.

	Gold	Blue	Light Plaid	Red
Row 1	7 Large	7 Medium	7 Small	—
Row 2	18 Large	18 Medium	—	18 Small
Row 3	24 Large	24 Small	24 Medium	—
Row 4	30 Small	30 Large	30 Medium	—
Row 5	36 Medium	36 Large	—	36 Small

Follow general directions for stitching your pennies together with the blanket stitch, attaching them to the base cloth and finishing the rug with the blanket stitch.

This table runner may take many hours of sewing pennies together, but it is pure joy to have it in the center of your table.

Hooked Rugs and Wool Appliqué

As I stated earlier in the book I started as a rug hooker and have continued with rug hooking. Rug hooking and penny rugs seem to go hand in hand and with creating penny rugs also comes wool appliqué. At times I will wool appliqué one of my rug hooking designs or use one of my wool appliqué designs for a hooked rug. Following are two examples of a design being hooked or appliquéd.

Who doesn't like pineapples and sheep? This tabletop rug was done as a Christmas present and hopefully it will welcome people for years to come.

Watermelon Feast

26 X 18.5

(See watermelon pattern, Page 58 and crows, Page 59)

Materials needed:

Red wool 12 X 6 inches.

Light Green wool 12 X 6 inches.

Dark Green wool 12 X 6 inches.

Black wool 25 X 6 inches.

Gold wool 20 X 3 inches.

 #5 Black Perle Coton, Gold Perle Coton.

Beige wool 26 X 18.5 inches for background

Backing same as front, or you can use flannel or homespun 26 X 18.5 inches.

Penny Rug Projects

If you are adding tongues you will need three layers, a circle, a background color wool, and black wool for the bottom layer of the tongue.

Red wool 12 X 1.5 inches for nine 1 inch wool circles.

Background beige wool for small tongue that measures 1.25 inches across and 2.5 inches long. Wool needed is 12 X 3 inches.

Black wool 24 X 3.5. The tongue is 2.5 inches across and 3 inches long.

Start by cutting out the watermelon pattern from the red, light green, and dark green. Place the dark green watermelon slice off center in the middle of your background wool, slightly tilted. Pin this in place and blanket stitch it in place, The light green slice is placed on top of the dark green but up a half inch so the dark green is showing. Before placing and stitching the red wool, cut out nine black seeds and either tack them on or blanket stitch them in place. Next the red watermelon slice is placed on top of the light green slice, again up a half inch so a small section of the light green shows. Pin it in place and blanket stitch around the red watermelon slice.

Cut out the three blackbirds and, using the picture for placement, place the birds around the watermelon slice. The eye is the gold Perle Coton and is two stitches on top of each other. The feet are the Gold Perle Coton using a straight stitch.

Cut out eight stars of various sizes. Place them around the crows and watermelon. Pin them in place and blanket stitch them onto the base wool. In a haphazardly way using the black Perle Coton and a running stitch go from to star to star and around the crows to help give the background a sense of movement.

If you are adding tongues, cut nine red circles, nine small tongues and nine large tongues. Make your own pattern tongue using a thin piece of cardboard. The small tongue is 1.25 inches across and 2.5 inches long, rounding off the bottom half. Blanket stitch a red circle onto the small tongue first, then blanket stitch the small tongue to the larger tongue. I did not blanket stitch around the black wool, but feel free to do so. After stitching all of the tongues together, I layered the front of the wool appliqué and the tongues to the back, pinned them all together and using a single running stitch, stitched it all together. You can use the blanket stitch if you prefer that instead.

Blackbird Pie

Shown hooked, 27 X 23.5 inches (See pattern, Page 58-59)

Materials needed:

Beige 48 X 6 inches

Gold 60 X 5 inches

Dark Plaid 15 X 3 inches

Dark Burgundy 30 X 3 inches

Black 60 X 12

Blue, four different shades of Blue each 30 X 10 inches.
(I had dyed four different light wools the same color for this background, but it would be just as stunning with different light, medium, and dark blue wool.

This is hooked with a #8 cut. Start with hooking the pie. The texture in the pie is swirls of gold and the pie opening is the dark plaid wool. The pie pan is Dark Burgundy. The crow's eye is a piece of gold cut in half lengthwise so the eye doesn't take up half of the head. The eye is the beginning of the strand, a loop and the end of the strand. The crow's wing is outlined with dark burgundy. The stars are gold with a single row of dark burgundy inside the star. To hook the background I followed the contour of the pie, crows and stars to help give the background movement. I also hooked "Blackbird Pie" into this rug. You can use writing or printing for the lettering at the bottom of your rug.

Although my love is for pennies, occasionally I will do a wool appliqué piece. I love to display this piece during the summer months when watermelon and crows are in abundance. I later hooked the same pattern, only changing the watermelon to a pie and calling the rug Blackbird Pie. At that time I was thinking of the nursery rhyme "four and twenty blackbirds baked in a pie".

*I designed this rug in a basic wool appliqué class
quite a few years ago. I love its primitiveness.*

Sheep in the Meadow
Shown appliquéd, 27.5 X 17.5
(see pattern, Page 61)

Materials needed:

Charcoal grey, two pieces 27.5 X 17.5 inches
for base wool and back; 40 X 16 inches for
tongues

Beige or off-white 15 X 6.5 inches

Green 12 X 10 inches

Blue 12 X 3 inches

Gold14 X 2.5 inches

Burgundy 12 X 5 inches

Gray Perle Coton #5, 2 skeins

Cut out the whole sheep in a single color. Make three pennies for each sheep with a half inch beige penny (same as the sheep) and a one-inch burgundy penny. Blanket stitch them to the sheep. Cut out the red heart, flower stems, and leaves. Pin the sheep, heart, stems, and leaves in place and blanket stitch them to the base wool. You can use a running stitch in the center of the stems instead of blanket stitching. Cut the gold for the center of the tulips and the blue tulips. Place and pin in place and blanket stitch them onto the base wool. Cut eight 1.5 inch gold circles and eight 1 inch burgundy circles. Blanket stitch together, place, pin, and blanket stitch to the base wool.

Cut out twenty four tongues, 3 inches across, 3.5 inches long. Make a pattern out of light cardboard and round off the end. Blanket stitch two tongues together. You will have twelve double tongues. Pin the tongues at each end sandwiching them between the front and the back. Following the directions for a tongue penny rug blanket stitch all around your wool appliqué rug.

Anne's Sheep

Shown hooked, 27.5 X 16
(see pattern, Page 60)

Materials needed:

Red 48 X 12 inches

Green Plaid 15 X 15 inches

Gold 15 X 10 inches

Blue 30 X 12 inches

Lt Beige 15 X 15 inches

Black 15 X 3 inches

Four different light green or beige wools,
    each 15 X 20 inches

I hooked the design just a little bit different
but the similarities are very much there.

This is hooked using a #8 cut. Start by hooking the heart
and the red tulip. Hook the stems and leaves and then the blue
tulips. Hook the gold in the middle of each tulip and the tiny circles
above each tulip. Hook the head, ear and legs of each sheep followed
by filling in the sheep. Hook a grass line under each sheep. Before hooking
in the background wool, hook a single line of blue all around the outside of the
pattern. Hook the background following the contour of the sheep, flowers and stems. I
had dyed four light colored wools the same color for the background but four different beige
wools would be just as nice. Hook two more rows of blue to complete the border.

The following two patterns are fun to hook and appliqué. The sheep rug even has pennies in its back ground and the flowers in The Pot of Posies are also sewn as pennies.

Sheep with Pennies

Shown hooked and appliquéd, 15 X 10
(See Pattern, Page 62)

These are two easy and quick projects. I have taught the hooked rug to beginner rug hookers.

Materials needed for hooking:

Oatmeal or light brown 15 X 3 inches

Beige 15 X 15 inches

Black 15 X 2 inches

Dark Blue 30 X 30 inches

Gold 15 X 7 inches

Bright blue 15 X 3 inches

Red 15 X 3 inches

Green 15 X 2.5 inches

This is hooked using a #8 cut. Hook the sheep's ear with black and then using the oatmeal or light brown hook the swirls inside the sheep. Before filling in the body of the sheep hook the sheep's face and legs with black, then fill in the sheep with the beige. The pennies are done with the various different colors. Fill in the background using a dark blue following the contour of the sheep and pennies.

Sheep are always very popular and since we deal with wool we like to have several rugs around to remind us where our joy comes from originally.

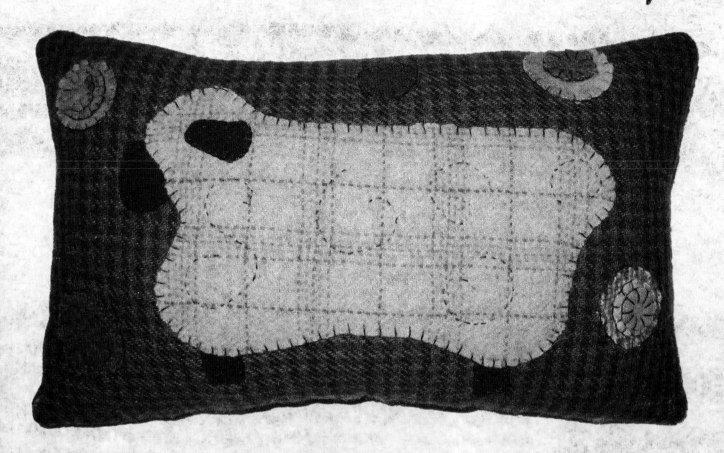

Materials needed for appliquéing:

Beige 10 X 7 inches

Scraps of multiple different colored circles

Black 4 X 4 scrap piece of wool

Dark Blue background, two pieces 14.5 X 7.5

1 skein black Perle Coton, #8 or #5

Using the blanket stitch appliqué the sheep onto the base wool. Using Black Perle Coton and a single running stitch to add swirls to the inside of the sheep. You can make two or three layer pennies using ½ inch pennies, 1 inch pennies, and 1 ½ inch pennies. Place them around the sheep and blanket stitch in place. Finish the appliqué by blanket stitching around the outside, or you can even make a pillow out of this appliqué.

Pot of Posies

Shown hooked and appliquéd, 12 X 12
(See Pattern, Page 63)

This pattern looks great either hooked or appliquéd. Making flowers out of pennies can bring out your creativity!

Materials needed for hooking:

Red 24 X 4 inches

Gold 14 X 3.5 inches

Green 15 X 15

Beige 30 X 6

Blue 30 X 6

Dark Brown Plaid 45 X 14

This is hooked in a #8 cut. Hook the flowerpot first with the beige. Outline the pot going all around the inside line. Start at the top and do two rows with the beige and then hook two rows of blue followed by the beige again to the bottom of the pot. Fill in the green leaves and stems, outlining the leaves. The flowers are gold centers and then two rows of red around the center. Before starting the background, hook one row around the border. Following the contour of the pot, leaves, and flowers fill in the background.

Hooked or appliquéd, this Pot of Posies will add warmth to your home as a small wall hanging or as a pillow.

Materials for appliqué:

Red 3 X 5 inches

Gold 3 X 2 inches

Green Plaid 9 X 7 inches

Beige 7 X 4.5

Blue 13.5 X 13.5

Dark Brown Plaid 50 X 24

Black Perle Coton, #8 or #5

Cutting the pot out of beige wool and, using a running stitch, appliqué a single strip of blue near the top of the pot. Blanket stitch this to the base wool. The stems and leaves are the green plaid. Appliqué the stems using the single running stitch, and blanket stitch the leaves. The flowers are like pennies, using the gold for the center and the red as the base of the flower. The piece can then be blanket stitched all around or made into a pillow.

Gallery

There are so many combinations of pennies and wool appliqué, you are only limited by your own imagination. Enjoy and have fun making your own Penny Rugs.

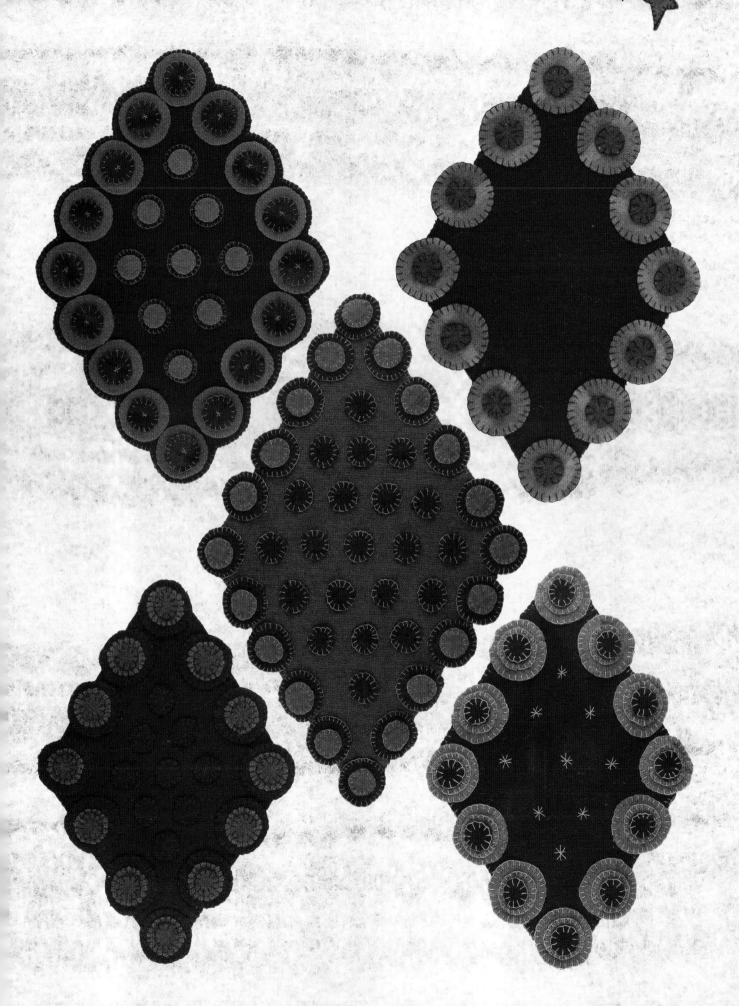

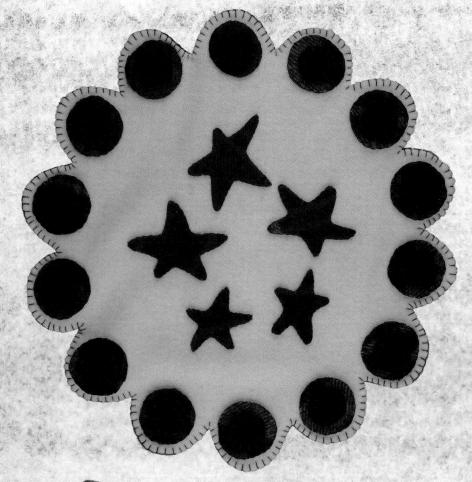

The small heart dish is by Foltz pottery, the brown mug by Stonesthrow Pottery.

Patterns and Templates

These are templates for patterns throughout the book.

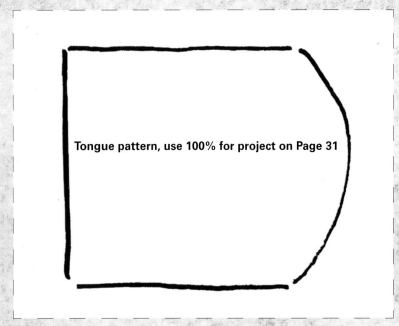

Tongue pattern, use 100% for project on Page 31

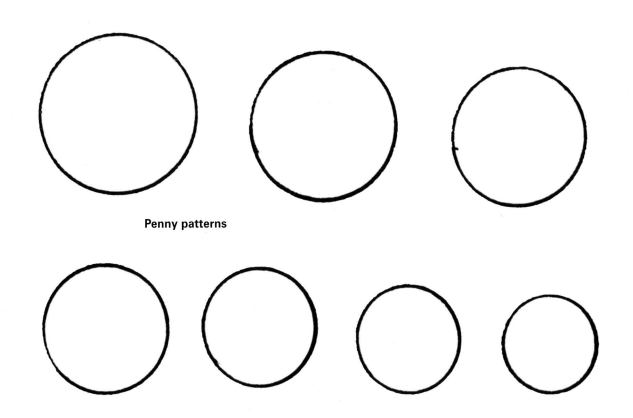

Penny patterns

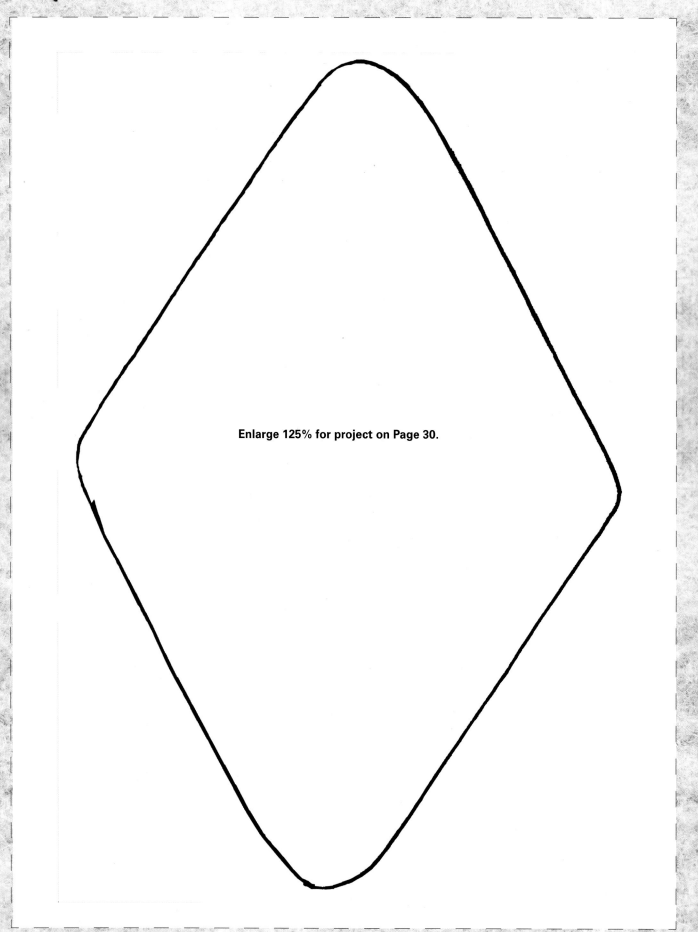

Enlarge 125% for project on Page 30.

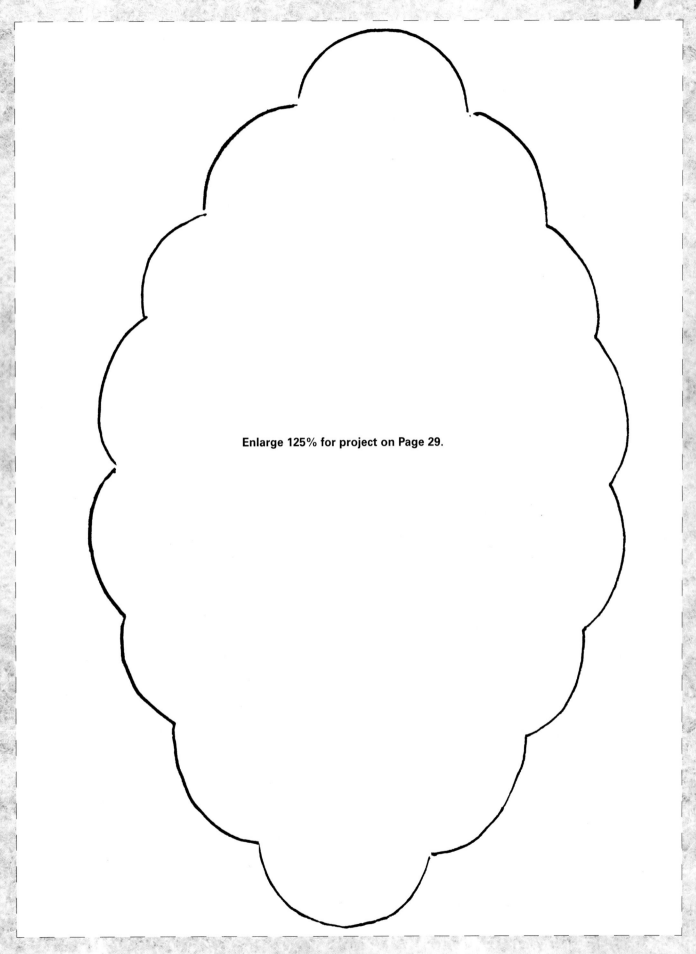

Enlarge 125% for project on Page 29.

This pattern is 100% for project on Page 28.

Enlarge 125% for project on Page 28.

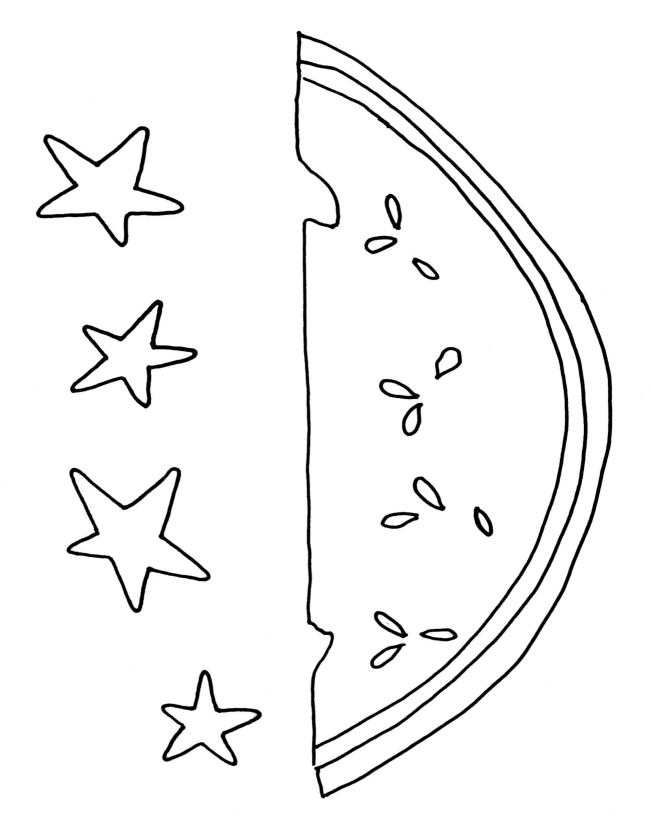

This pattern is 100% for project on Page 37.

This pattern is 100% for project on Pages 37 & 39.

Enlarge 125 % for project on Page 41.

These pattern pieces are 100% for project on Page 40.

sheep's ear

sheep's face

sheep's legs

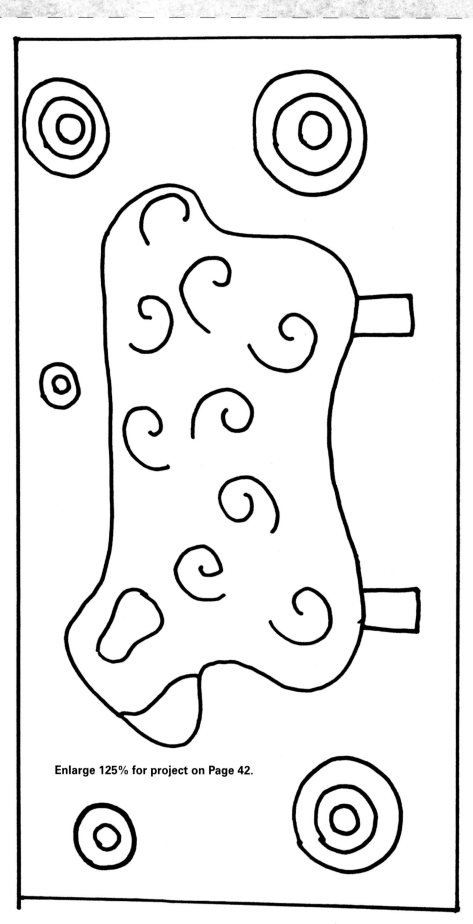

Enlarge 125% for project on Page 42.

This pattern is 100% for project on Page 44.

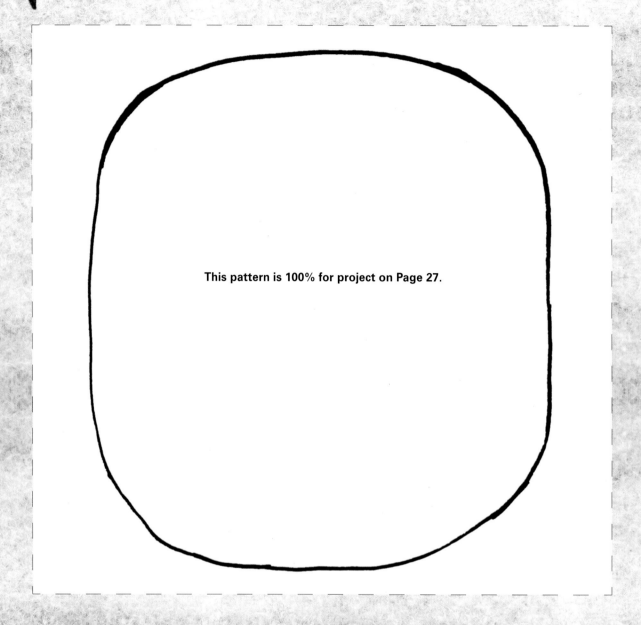

This pattern is 100% for project on Page 27.

Bibliography

Hicks, Any Mali. *The Craft of Hand-Made Rugs.* New York: McBride, Nast, & Company. 1914.

Walker, Lydia LeBaron. *Homecraft Rugs.* New York; Frederick A. Stokes Company. 1929.

Suppliers

There are many wonderful wool shops dotted all over the country that supply both wool, lessons, and encouragement. Be sure to support your local craft store. Additionally, there are two major wholesale/retail suppliers that help feed the needs of rug hookers and crafters around the country. They are:

The Dorr Mill Store, P.O. Box 88, Guild, NH 03754, 800-846-3677, www.doormillstore.com.

The Wool Studio, 706 Brownsville Road, Sinking Spring, PA 19608 610-678-5448, www.thewoolstudio.com.